Grief Notes:
An Invitation to Honor Your Grieving Process

Dani Hickman

Copyright © 2021 by Danielle Hickman

All rights reserved.

No part of this book may be reproduced in any form or by any electronic or mechanical means, including information storage and retrieval systems, without written permission from the author, except for the use of brief quotations in a book review.

Cover design by: Cassidy Rae Marietta
Author photo by: Tillie Lee

ISBN: 978-0-578-97077-6

DEDICATION

For my dad.
With you here, this book would have never been written.

FOREWORD

Dear Friend,

If you have found your way to this book it means you are experiencing tremendous heartache.

Know that I am sending you love.

My hope is that this compilation of my personal grief notes will support you in your journey as you learn how to honor and navigate your own grief.

That the words on these pages will be a companion throughout your healing journey—an energetic presence as you learn how to be present with your grief.

Use these words as a guide—a tool to illuminate parts of the grieving process you may be unable to see in this moment.

In writing these words, I am witnessing and honoring my own pain resulting from the unexpected loss of my father. As I experience this loss, I recognize that without a deep love, we cannot experience a deep loss. These grief notes are a reminder of my deep love for my father.

It is an honor to hold space for you,

Dani

gracefully grieving

I meet my grieving process with grace, not judgment.

reminders

When my grief is triggered,
I choose to see it as a beautiful reminder
of my love for you.

innate wisdom

I allow my system to guide me in the grieving process.

    My mind and body hold an innate wisdom
    to move toward healing and wholeness.

check-in with yourself

I don't expect others to know what I need.
I spend intentional time with myself to check-in with my mind, body and spirit.

just notice

When I feel consumed by my thoughts,
I shift my attention to my body.
I notice what my feet feel like on the floor.
I notice what it feels like to be supported by
the chair on which my body is resting.

I invite myself to take a few deep breaths as I notice what
it feels like to be fully supported by the chair with no
expectation to work hard in this moment.

I am at peace knowing that I do not have to try or do
anything in this moment—
I allow the chair to fully support me.

let the present moment support you

When I feel lost, I reconnect with my present moment. I notice my surroundings—focusing on what I see, hear, smell and touch in this moment.

your pain deserves expression

        In this moment, I honor my pain.
I do this by allowing free expression of my emotions.

our love runs deep

It is a beautiful thing to experience the feeling of loss—
it means I have experienced a deep love.

there you are

Instead of "You left me."
I choose curiosity and explore, "Where are you?"
And I look for reminders of you around me.
I allow myself to feel the love in my body when I notice,

"There you are."

Dani Hickman

presence

I do my best to be present in the memory of you.
Even when it hurts, I choose *presence*.

(it doesn't need to a look a certain way)

        I allow myself to grieve without expectation.

an invitation

I tune into my body and ask myself,

"What do I need in this moment to feel supported?"

Food?

Rest?

A scream?

A good cry?

Laughter?

A cuddle?

not today, paul

I give myself permission to set boundaries.

boundaries are love

Boundaries are an expression of love.
My boundaries communicate *I love myself and I love you*
enough to fully express what I can
and
cannot do in this moment.

(you can take up space)

I allow myself to express what I need
and do not need in this moment.

I also give myself permission to *not know* what I need.

let it rip

When I feel angry, I give myself permission to channel
this anger into something that serves me.
I explore healthy expressions of anger
and allow my system to release this energy.

Sometimes I need to rage—so, I rage.

life isn't fair

When I feel my loss is unfair, I give myself permission
(without judgment)
to express these words.

Dani Hickman

emotions need motion

I support the processing of my emotions.
I am present with the emotions in my body
and give them permission to move.
I create the space for my emotions
to have the *motion* they desire.

They will move when they're ready.

I feel you everywhere

I lean into the deep knowing that
I am a spiritual being having a human experience.
Anchored in this knowledge,
I remind myself that you are
no longer confined to a human body—
you have re-emerged into pure spirit.

And what a beautiful thing for you to be everywhere all at once.

death is a transition

I mourn the loss of your physical presence,
but connect with my ability to have
a continued, nonphysical relationship with you.
I am at peace knowing that I can access you at any
moment in time by tuning into your energy
and the essence of you.

Because the soul is infinite.

I choose love

I look for reminders of you.
It feels good to be reminded of
the love shared between us.

(you can shift your focus)

In this moment, I choose gratitude.

grief is exhausting

I give myself permission to rest.

I choose to show up for myself

I allow my body to communicate its needs to me.
I cultivate a loving relationship with myself
by listening to and meeting these needs.

scream machine

I give myself permission to scream.

no one knows what they're doing

I will not confine my grieving process to
a box of expectations.
I will offer myself permission to
grieve in a way that supports me,
releasing pressure to grieve in
a way that makes others comfortable.
I will allow my grieving process to
be whatever it needs to be,
giving grief *the movement* it needs to heal.

(because the alternative will eat me alive)

I choose to see the beauty in my grief.

Dani Hickman

take time for yourself

I take time for solitude
and allow this space to replenish me.

move forward

I continue to move forward despite the pain.
I allow my pain to be a companion
along my journey forward.

let love in

I allow myself to be supported by those who love me.

(open for cuddles)

I give myself permission to
ask others to give me what I need…

Can you just hold me?

the questions won't go away

I am present in the questions that do not have answers.
I offer myself peace in the unknown.

Why you?
Why now?
What will I do now?
What could I have done differently?
Could I have stopped this?

be still

In the stillness,
I find grief.
In this stillness,
I also find myself.

Dani Hickman

(we're all doing the best we can)

I offer love to others—
even when they do not know how to support me.
In these moments, I use this as an invitation
to support myself.

some days are a 2/10

I give myself grace and simply do the best I can.
I give myself permission to allow this to ebb and flow.

(being mean to yourself doesn't help)

I offer myself grace and compassion as
I learn how to sit with my grief.

allow the calm to enter

I invite peace into my experience.
I do not judge myself when
a sense of calm enters into my grieving process.

Dani Hickman

spinning my wheels

When I feel overwhelmed,
I slow down and anchor into my body.

lean into the emptiness

When I feel empty, I connect with this emptiness
and learn how to be present in this vast space.
I don't run from the emptiness…

I learn how to inhabit it.

Dani Hickman

dancing with grief

I move my body to allow space for
the energy of grief to move.
I learn how to dance with my grief—
seeing my grief as a partner in the moment,
not an enemy.

stay curious

I stay curious,
allowing this curiosity to guide my grief journey.

let love guide you

When I feel lost, I connect with love.
I remind myself that I have the choice
to reconnect with the energy of love at any moment.

(feeling better is a choice)

I have the power to shift my thinking to support my journey forward.

helpless

If I feel like a victim,
I acknowledge this younger part of me.
I support this part by being curious and asking:
"How can I help you?"

(the numbness is an invitation)

When I feel numb, I use this as an invitation
to reconnect with my body.
I use my hands to make slow contact with my vessel.
Through this process, I invite myself safely back into
intentionally inhabiting my body.

Dani Hickman

you can learn to feel safe in the unknown

When I am experiencing the unknown,
I focus on taking one step forward at a time.

denial is a part of the process

When denial feels deep,
I allow myself to wade in the waters.

(this is what you would have wanted)

I give myself permission to feel good.

make friends with your fear

When I feel fear, I learn how to sit in this space.
Hello, fear. I see you.
Welcome.

(my grief isn't here to make you comfortable)

I allow myself to feel what is present in the moment
regardless of what is deemed "acceptable."
I remind myself it is not my job
to make others comfortable with my grieving process.

don't let your logical brain block your processing

When I feel stuck in my emotions,
I drop below my logical stories
and open the dialogue with my emotional self.
I notice my thoughts and invite myself
to tune into my body.
What am I *feeling* in my body
when I think these thoughts?

Dani Hickman

we all love a good distraction

I notice when I am distracting myself and
tune back into my body and present experience.

And, sometimes,
I give myself permission to distract.

duality

I understand the duality of the human experience.
In order to experience life,
I must become acquainted with death.
To fully experience love,
I must become acquainted with loss.

Dani Hickman

(don't abandon your inner child)

Feelings of abandonment are
my inner child asking for comfort.
I ask my inner child,
"What do you need to feel safe right now?

allow space for the loneliness

When I feel lonely, I spend time exploring this vast space.
I learn how to be present in the void.

your emotions are safe

When I feel fearful of being present in my emotions,
I imagine myself comforting my inner child.
I remind my inner child that I am an adult now.
I have the ability to feel my feelings and
stay safe in the processing of my grief.

I can trust myself

I allow my body to experience the waves of grief, fully trusting that my system will support me in the processing, healing, and releasing of this grief.

Dani Hickman

let the waters move

I allow my emotions to flow like the river.
I acknowledge that when I restrict the flow,
the river feels unmanageable as the waters rise.

let's rage

When I feel rage,
I invite healthy expression of this rage.
I give my inner child permission to scream, yell, and jump up
        and
                down.

Dani Hickman

(it's okay to miss you)

When I think of moments
you won't be present to witness,
                        I honor this feeling of loss.

reframe

When I experience a moment when
I wish you were here,
I take a breath and attune to what it would feel like to
experience this moment *with you*.

Dani Hickman

abundant in love

When I feel overwhelmed with my loss,
I witness and honor this pain.
Then I choose to shift my focus to the
abundance of the love we shared.

(it can still be a celebration)

On holidays, I celebrate with you.

Dani Hickman

make room for good days

Today is a good day.
You would remind me of that.

                      I can choose to experience a good day
                          while also honoring my grief.

(your body knows how to process emotions)

I choose to intentionally inhabit my body—
allowing the space for my emotions to naturally flow.

take care of yourself

Today I give myself the gift of self-care and compassion.
I attune to myself to see what I need
and how I can support myself.

Grief Notes

(no one wins this comparison)

> I don't compare my grieving process to
> the process of others.

allow your emotions to be present without reason

I recognize my desire to understand my loss logically.
I offer myself permission to experience my emotions
without a logical understanding of
where they come from.

goodbye, future tripping

> When I feel fear about the future,
> I reconnect with the present moment.

Dani Hickman

(my authentic self is so sad)

To deny my feelings of grief is to
gag the expression of my authentic self.

just feel it

When I question the validity of my emotions,
I open the door to suffering.

Dani Hickman

(it takes courage to be present in your pain)

With courage, I name my pain.
I allow myself to witness the emotions
calling for my attention.

stop the self-imposed suffering, friend

In my grieving process emotional pain is inevitable.

                        Suffering, however, is optional.

Dani Hickman

I can choose to anchor in the energy of love

When I feel stuck in my grief,
I remember I have control over my focus and attention.

> I choose love.
> Always love.

(learn how to ride the wave)

I ride the waves of grief
        and look for the beauty in the process.

Dani Hickman

(your body is an expert in processing grief)

When I feel suspicious that I will never
move through my grief, I remind myself
my body has been designed to process emotions.

resilience

I am resilient.
I do not have to "try" to be resilient.
It is in my nature.

just keep swimming…

When I notice myself drowning in despair,
I actively choose to start swimming toward shore.

how can I support myself?

I acknowledge that this hurts like hell.
I also choose to explore what I need to
move through this pain in the moment.

allow the flow of your emotions

I am flexible with my process.

I cry.

I'm angry.

I'm happy.

I cry again.

I feel peace.

who am I without you?

I acknowledge a piece of me is gone—but I lean into the parts of my identity that still exist and make me

who I am.

(even when I don't want to...)

I give myself space to adapt to life without you.

old behaviors die hard

Sometimes you'll find yourself moving toward
old behaviors to cope with your grief.
You left those behaviors long ago
because they did not serve you.

Beware of the whispers of grief that tell you otherwise.

witness your pain

Your inner child will need to grieve.
Spend time with this part of yourself.
Be curious, be present.
Give them permission to grieve.
They are only a child, after all.

(you can't run forever)

You may feel like running from your grief—
not wanting to be present in the full, messy experience.
As you run from yourself, you may find yourself
physically walking out the door—
running away from those willing to
hold space (and you) in your process.
Remember to breathe—
invite yourself back into your body.
Remind yourself that it is safe to
be seen and held in your grief.

you're pure magic

Being present in your body with your grief
can feel overwhelming and heavy.

Moments when you are so physically depleted,
opening your eyes feels like work.

Give yourself permission to lean into this exhaustion.
Notice the heaviness of grief that is present in your body.

Breathe into these spaces and acknowledge your body is
working hard to process and release this energy.

Show this heaviness love,
it's a reminder of the magical things your body can do.

professional napper

There is no such thing as too many naps.

Rest.

Your body is working hard.

Dani Hickman

overflowing abundance

It's hard to "benefit" from your death.
You died and I gained access to financial abundance.
I think to myself, if you could come back,
I would give it all up.

But, you can't.

In this moment, I choose to lean into how you continue to bless me with your love.

I am abundant because your love was abundant.

the new reality

It feels like a dream.
Did that just happen?
Are you really gone?
My mind feels foggy, confused.

But the ache in my heart gives me clarity.
It is true—you are gone…
But I don't want to accept it.

I show this part of me love.

Dani Hickman

(try to keep your heart open)

A part of me wants to feel alone and not share my grief.
My ego tries to keep me separate and tell me
no one can understand my pain.
But I remind myself that I can give them
an opportunity to try.

grief is always unfolding

I grieve for the future moments—
the moments you'll miss.
I remind myself that despite
the lack of your physical presence,
I will always have the connection to who you were—
your energy, your personality, your humor.

Dani Hickman

return to sender

People send letters.
They are well-meaning,
full of their own grief experiences....
But not mine.
Well intentioned, but they fall short.

> It's okay to not find them helpful.
> *Thanks anyway.*

(terrible, thanks for asking)

Grief makes people uncomfortable.
They ask, "How are you?"
Secretly hoping you'll simply answer, "fine."

Being present with someone in their pain isn't easy.
But neither is the excruciating pain of grief.

Dani Hickman

I still hate you, small talk

Dear small talk,

Just don't.

Seriously…don't.

(can you come back now?)

Support comes in the form of
lasagnas, casseroles and cookies.

Well-meaning statements of,
"Let me know what you need…"

…my dad.

(the things you want to say…but don't)

"Let me know what I can do for you."
Nothing, unless you can bring my dad back.

"My heart breaks for you."
Does it? Well imagine my heart.

"I don't know what to say."
Then shut up.

"I'm shocked!"
…I don't care.

pleading

>Dear Grim Reaper,
>
>Could you take _____ instead?
>
>Much obliged.

Dani Hickman

it feels like a daze

The memory of your face keeps surprising me.
As time passes, I still find myself asking,
"Is this even real?"

depressed

Life feels harder now.

I look at the dishes in the sink…nope.
I look at my to-do list…nope.
I look at my work schedule…please, don't make me.
I look at my bed…yes, please.

how to not be ugly

Ugly cries can't be ugly if no one is watching.

(Sometimes I want to be alone in my pain).

conversations with you

I talk to you more now than when you were alive.
I think of your opening line, "What do I need to know?"
And then proceed to tell you
everything you need to know…
And then some.

I *choose* to feel close to you.

Dani Hickman

asking for a friend

Dear God,

Can my dad see *everything* I do now that he's in heaven?

Please tell him to knock before entering,

Slightly concerned daughter

ACKNOWLEDGMENTS

Francis Weller speaks to the importance of healing grief within the village—inviting in support of your community and loved ones to hold you in your vulnerability and depths of grief. Thank you to my village for seeing me, holding me and witnessing me in my grief.

More specifically, I would like to thank my big sister, Jenny Fyfe, for her guidance in making this book a reality—for the obnoxious check-ins about my self-imposed deadlines, the pep talks to not hide and give up and, of course, sharing the wisdom that "your first draft will always be shit." To my sister, Megan Kitzmiller and my mom, thank you for holding space for me throughout this year and for continuing to be a support when our family system traumatically shifted.

To my other sister, Tillie Lee, for being my space-holder, truth-teller and "down to cry" best friend—this shared experience is not ideal, but a sacred sisterhood to me. To Adam Roth, thank you for loving all parts of me and supporting me as grief invites me to continuously unfold into my next level of becoming—and, for not letting me give up on the words on these pages.

ABOUT THE AUTHOR

Dani Hickman is a Psychotherapist & Embodiment Coach living in Nashville, Tennessee dedicated to living a life of integrity: *a life that is whole, integrated and undivided.*

To her, this means she is living in alignment with her most authentic self—both inwardly and outwardly. She's invested in her own trauma healing and recovery of self—exploring the depths of who she is and becoming reacquainted with the parts of her that have been abandoned along her own life's journey.

She considers herself a *Soul Activist*, doing what she can to support and guide others on how to move through the world from a soul-aligned place—anchored in their body and in tune with their inner guidance system.

Dani is traditionally trained as a Trauma Psychotherapist and Usui Tibetan Reiki Master. She has experience providing trauma psychotherapy in a wide variety of settings including private practice, in-home, schools, the mission field, inpatient and outpatient settings.

Over the last decade, she has gained extensive experience supporting the healing of individuals with a history of trauma. She has received advanced training in trauma-informed therapeutic modalities such as: Cognitive Behavioral Therapy, Trauma Focused Cognitive Behavioral Therapy, Eye Movement Desensitization and Reprocessing (EMDR), Inner Child Work and Brainspotting.

When she's not working, you'll find her hiking on a mountain or at the base of a waterfall, at an antique store or obsessively reading on personal and spiritual growth topics. Or, in a perfect world, she's listening to a spiritual growth audiobook while making pit stops at antique stores along the journey to a great hike.

CPSIA information can be obtained
at www.ICGtesting.com
Printed in the USA
LVHW011217310322
714806LV00007B/1383